Getting Free from the Curse of Vashti [FOR WOMEN]

Ebenezer & Abigail
Gabriels

Ebenezer & Abigail Gabriels
19644 Club House Road Suite 815
Gaithersburg, Maryland 20886
www.EbenezerGabriels.Org
hello@ebenezergabriels.org

DEDICATION

Your testimony to the Son of God, is the spirit of
prophecy.
Your testimony is made known through the power of your
revelation. Every of the insights, revelation and power you
are releasing through this book is to the glory of your
Holy name, JESUS, and for the deliverance of women and
families across the earth.

CONTENT

1

~

THE SUCCESS OF VASHTI

Queen Vashti is long gone, but the spirit of Vasht is very much around today. The spirit of Vashti is one not to allow in, and the curse of Vashti is one of the curses today's christian women need to break over their lives. This spirit is a subtle but ravaging spirit, and its end goal is to push women into desolation, barrenness and loneliness.

The spirit of Vashti is not prominent when the woman has not attained success. Not much is heard about the spirit of Vashti before a marriage, or before Vashti enters into a position of prominence. This spirit may put on false humility to get the commitment of marriage from a man. This spirit may trick a man into marriage, and displays false humility to get the title of wife. This spirit may also feign humility in an organization to climb the ladders of success. Once she gets the success she's hoped for, as defined by her. The spirit of Vashti begins to manifest. This curse awaits the time of success of the woman and seeks to pull her down into desolation.

Esther 1:9
Queen Vashti also made a feast for the women in the royal palace which belonged to King Ahasuerus.

Vashti was the wife of King Ahasuerus. There, at the peak of her office as queen, a curse was awaiting her at the top. The curse of Vashti is one of the curses particularly attacks any reasonable relationship that may lead to marriage, or the marriage itself of successful women if not broken.

Unknowingly to the spiritually unaware women, after success in career, marriage, ministry or in another domain, the spirit of Vashti may creep in.

THE ROLE OF QUEEN VASHTI

Vashti would have continued to be the queen if she understood her role. The lack of understanding of her role was the beginning of her downfall. If Vashti had asked, "Lord, what is my purpose"? She might have received understanding of what her calling was. Vashti was called into queenhood. In her office as queen, her role and office works alongside, helping the king. The role of Vashti is explained below:

1. The role of the queen is not the female version of the king.
2. Without an established kingdom, there is no position of the king, hence no queen
3. The kingdom has to do with the kingdom of a king

4. The queen will see much success in her position as a queen, not as a king. The spirit of Vashti is a spirit of success

HOW THE SPIRIT OF VASHTI IS PERVERTED AND BECOMES THE CURSE UPON VASHTI

The success of Vashti represents the height of success a woman may get into in any domain, especially marriage. In career, women advance high. However, the spirit of Vashti is a spirit that targets successful women, and seeks to bring them to the ground.

The Spirit of Vashti in Marriage

In marriage, the spirit of Vashti is at work in vulnerable women who are in prominent marriages to bring them down and leave them forgotten in their marriages. This curse is also hidden in plain sight and responsible for some women advanced in age unable to find a husband.

The Spirit of Vashti in Ministry

In ministry, the spirit of Vashti may creep into the lives of vulnerable women in successful ministries and leave them forgotten in their ministries. Within the church, this spirit seeks spiritually vulnerable women and casts them out of their ministries. When the spirit of Vashti is within a church, the Spirit of Vashti is anti-kingdom, they want to divide the kingdom of God by building their own mini-thing especially because it appears to be a type of success they think they could leverage.

The Spirit of Vashti in Organization

Within an organization, the spirit of Vashti works when a woman who holds an important position begins to hold the organization ransom because of her success in different areas. She might have established herself as the leader in a process in the workplace, suddenly, because of her success, she distances herself from the success of the organization but begins to build her own mini-organization within the organization.

THE END GAME OF THE SPIRIT OF VASHTI

This spirit targets successful vulnerable women. It does not target unsuccessful women. The goal of this spirit is to invite curses upon these women to bring them to the ground and leave them forgotten. The endgame of the Spirit of Vashti is to strip powerful women off their royal seat and replace them with what they have considered irrelevant. The spirit of Vashti seeks to cast powerful and successful women into irrelevance, especially in marriage. Where relevance is stolen from the rightful woman in a marriage, watch out for the spirit of vashti.

PRAYERS OF DELIVERANCE FROM THE SPIRIT OF SUCCESS LACED WITH FAILURE

WORSHIP DECREE

On the altar of worship to Yahweh
The power of the Holy Ghost come down
The spirit of power come down
To consume the sacrifice of worship
Fire from heaven fall

MEDITATE

Collosians 2- 11::15

In Him you were also circumcised with the circumcision made without hands, by putting off the body of the sins of the flesh, by the circumcision of Christ, 12buried with Him in baptism, in which you also were raised with Him through faith in the working of God, who raised Him from the dead. 13And you, being dead in your trespasses and the uncircumcision of your flesh, He has made alive together with Him, having forgiven you all trespasses, 14having wiped out the handwriting of requirements that was against us, which was contrary to us. And He has taken it out of the way, having nailed it to the cross. 15Having disarmed principalities and powers, He made a public spectacle of them, triumphing over them in it..

PRAYERS OF DELIVERANCE FROM THE SPIRIT OF SUCCESS ALIGNED WITH FAILURE

1. Curses of Vashti awaiting me at the top, be broken by the blood of Jesus
2. Curses of Vashti awaiting me at the roadside, be broken by the blood of Jesus
3. Curses of Vashti awaiting the me at the junction of success be broken down by the blood of Jesus,
4. Spirit of pride, seeking to bring the curse of Vashti upon me, be uprooted from my life in the name of Jesus
5. In the place of prominence, the spirit of Vashti shall have no hold over my life in the name of Jesus.
6. The spirit of Vashti shall not locate me in my career in the name of Jesus
7. The spirit of Vashti shall find no entry point in me in the name of Jesus
8. The spirit of Vashti shall not locate me in my marriage in the name of Jesus
9. The spirit of Vashti shall not locate me in my ministry in the name of Jesus.
10. Failure shall have no place in the success the Lord has given to me.
11. Failure shall not be a marker in my success, in the name of Jesus.
12. My ministry success shall not work in partnership with the spirit of failure in the name of Jesus

13. My marriage shall not partner with the spirit of failure in the name of Jesus

14. My career success shall not partner with the spirit of failure in the name of Jesus.

15. My testimony will not be soiled in the name of Jesus

16. The spirit of Vashti shall not inhabit my life int the name of Jesus.

JOURNAL

2

~

THE SPIRIT OF FALSE INDEPENDENCE

The spirit of Vashti is responsible for the false independence manifested in the lives of those whom it is at work. The spirit of Vashti feels self sufficient and is responsible for married women seeking to step away from their God-given role. Satan uses the desire for false independence as a tool to lure women out of the companionship of their marriage, or out of the desire to get married.

Esther 1:10-12

On the seventh day, when the heart of the king was merry with wine, he commanded Mehuman, Biztha, Harbona, Bigtha, Abagtha, Zethar, and Carcas, seven eunuchs who served in the presence of King Ahasuerus, to bring Queen

Vashti before the king, wearing her royal crown, in order to show her beauty to the people and the officials, for she was beautiful to behold. But Queen Vashti refused to come at the king's command brought by his eunuchs; therefore the king was furious, and his anger burned within him.

No one is designed to be self-sufficient. Couples need each other. When a husband or wife begins to think they are self-sufficient, pride has set in, and they begin to make rules based on the perception of fasle independence.

HOW THE SPIRIT OF FALSE INDEPENDENCE WORKS
The spirit of false independence pushes into pride. It may manifest in the following ways:

#1: Mentality of Independence
This spirit pushes some unmarried sisters into a new mentality of independence that they think they have no need for marriage.

#2. Underestimating others
This spirit pushes some unmarried ladies to underestimate the man they send their way. They speak to people in a lowly way.

#3 No Need to Marry
It can manifest in ladies who advanced in age, and have resorted they do not need to get married because of the hurts and heartbreaks they have undergone

#4 I Earn More than You

It can manifest in a woman that is married to a man who is earning less and she assumes she is the independent one.

#5 Burning Bridges after any Little Success

When the spirit of vashti encounters a tiny appearance of success, pride overshadows Vashit and Vashi begins to burn the bridges. The spirit of Vashti forgets where she is coming from, after some success, the Spirit of Vashti becomes prideful towards her spouse, or those who have been influential to her rising.

#6 Dishonor Authority

When the spirit of Vashti encounters success, Vashti disrespects and dishonors those in a position of authority. Vashti prides herself so much in her connections that Vashti dishonors authority, because she is in the place of authority herself.

#7 Prides itself in Beauty

The spirit of Vashti prides itself in the beauty of the one whom it has held captive. The spirit of Vashti pushes a vulnerable woman to misbehave. The spirit of Vashti uses her beauty as her tool of negotiation in marriage or relationships.

#8 Marital Sex for Manipulation

The spirit of Vashti is the spirit responsible for wives manipulating with the instrument of sex. The spirit of Vashti says to the husband, my body no longer belongs to you.

#9 Misbehaving at the Sight of Success

The spirit of Vashti, when it attains any form of success, misbehaves. When Vashti smells success, she begins to further her personal agenda and association, dishonoring the established order of God in her life

#10 Easy Offended

This spirit manifests women who are vulnerable to the spirit of pride. Within the church, an offense is easily taken, it could be the way someone seated next to them spoke to them, they proclaim an independence from the body of Christ.

#10 Not Building With You

The spirit of Vashti is against building together. If the spirit of Vashti is at work in a marriage, the wife would not build with the husband. The spirit of Vashti does not want to partake in building a vision, but wants to engage in frivolous spending and is over-entitled. The spirit of Vashti would not partake in building her God-given vision, but would seek to build "her own thing", activities which eventually leads into fruitlessness.

THE PROGRESSION OF THE CURSE OF VASHTI

The spirit of false independence manifests in many ways, much more than mentioned above. Once the spirit of Vashti kicks into women, there would be manifestations of different types. This false independence spirit usually leads to major errors opening ways for inescapable curses. Also, the spirit of Vashti waits at the peak of offices, to bring great falls

PRAYERS OF DELIVERANCE FROM THE SPIRIT OF FALSE INDEPENDENCE

WORSHIP DECREE

On the altar of worship to Yahweh
The power of the Holy Ghost come down
The spirit of power come down
To consume the sacrifice of worship
Fire from heaven fall

MEDITATE

Jeremiah 2- 28
In Him But where are your gods that you have made for yourselves? Let them arise, If they can save you in the time of your trouble; For according to the number of your cities Are your gods, O Judah

Proverbs 3:5
Trust in the Lord with all your heart, And lean not on your own understanding

PRAYERS FOR DELIVERANCE FROM THE SPIRIT OF FALSE INDEPENDENCE

1. Lord Jesus, You are my sufficiency in the name of Jesus
2. Every garment of pride upon my life, be taken off in the name of Jesus

3. Lord, cloth me with your garment of power and glory in the name of Jesus

4. Lord, deliver me from the spirit of deception in the name of Jesus

5. Lord, let my complete independence on you in the name of Jesus.

6. I bring my entire life into the name of the Lord, in the name of Jesus

7. My beauty shall not become vanity in the name of Jesus

8. Powers of pride at work in my life, be uprooted in the name of Jesus

9. Spirit of pride, pushing me into desolation, be cast out of my destiny in the name of Jesus

10. Spirit of reliance on self, be cast out of my life in the name of Jesus

11. Spirit of reliance on status, be cast out of my life in the name of Jesus

12. Spirit of reliance on fame, be cast out of my life in the name of Jesus.

13. Spirit of reliance on accomplishments, be cast out of my life in the name of Jesus.

14. Spirit of reliance on financial powers, be cast out of my life in the name of Jesus.

15. Spirit of pride in its entirety, bringing me into enmity with God, be uprooted from my foundation in the name of Jesus.

JOURNAL

3

~

THE SPIRIT OF ERROR

The curse of Vashti goes hand in hand with the spirit of error which brings judgement. in high places with kings, princes and rulers. Where there is the curse of Vashti, the spirit of error is nearby. This curse pushes vulnerable women into irrecoverable error. This is why some people fall into error in the most critical time and errs in high places against kings, rulers and authorities.

Vashti's husband was a king. He occupied the highest seat in the land. Every king and leader in the place of authority is a representative of God. The authority a king uses is of God, hence anyone who defies that authority faces the judgement of God

---

Romans 13:1-2

> Let every soul be subject to the governing authorities. For there is no authority except from God, and the authorities that exist are appointed by God. Therefore whoever resists the authority resists

the ordinance of God, and those who resist will bring
judgment on themselves

HOW THE SPIRIT OF ERROR AGAINST AUTHORITY OCCURS IN MARRIAGE

There's an authority over men in marriage that comes from God. When the authority of God over the life of a woman is ridiculed over the life of a man by his wife, the Lord does not take it lightly.

1. The spirit of error is shown in the life of the woman who ridicules her husband in public square.
2. The spirit of error is manifested in the life of the woman who pulls her husband down with her words

THE SPIRIT OF VASHTI AND THE SPIRIT OF ERROR I
The spirit of false independence pushes into pride. It may manifest in the following ways:

#1: Error at the Moment of Worship
Vashti's beauty was the works of God. Vashit's husband had observed and studied Vashti's beauty. He was going to show forth God's creativity in his wife but Vashti lacked this understanding and denied her husband the opportunity to delight in God's work.

1. When your husband seeks to appreciate your beauty, this is as worship unto the Lord
2. There's no shame in a spouse delighting in the beauty of another.

#2: Error of Withholding Affection in Marriage

The spirit of Vashti brings along the spirit of error. Where the spirit of Vashti pushes the woman to withhold the affection due to her husband, the husband is prone to the error and temptation as seen in 1 Corinthians 7: 5-6 *Do not deprive one another except with consent for a time, that you may give yourselves to fasting and prayer; and come together again so that Satan does not tempt you because of your lack of self-control.*

#3: Error of Hindering Worship

This same spirit of Vashti was at work in the life of Michal, the first wife of king David when she said to her husband:

2 Samuel 6:20
"Then David returned to bless his household. And Michal the daughter of Saul came out to meet David, and said, How glorious was the king of Israel today, uncovering himself today in the eyes of the maids of his servants, as one of the base fellows shamelessly uncovers himself!"

Micah was also a royal. She was a princess, and also a queen. Yet she despised the worship her husband gave to God. Because worship is so precious to God, the angels of God does not take lightly anything or anyone that seeks to hinder worship.

2 Samuel 6:21-23

So David said to Michal, "It was before the Lord, who chose me instead of your father and all his house, to appoint me ruler over the people of the Lord, over Israel. Therefore I will play music before the Lord. And I will be even more *undignified than this, and will be humble in my own sight. But as for the maidservants of whom you have spoken, by them I will be held in honor." Therefore Michal the daughter of Saul had no children to the day of her death.*

The curse of Vashti lures into the error that seeks to mock the worship of others and display pride towards God. Michal was prideful and despised how her husband worshipped God. This spirit is directly in opposition with God and brings the instant judgment of God, and the curse of unfruitfulness.

#4: Error Against a Community

When this error occurs, the magnitude of the punishment is always as though the woman has sinned against the highest leader in the land, regardless of her husband's status in the society. This same spirit was at work in the life of Michal, the first wife of king David when she said to her husband, who erred against her husband as he was dancing alongside other worshippers.

The woman of God must continue to pray that this wicked spirit that seeks to ruin women will not stand a chance in her life. The woman carrying God's glory must continue to rebuke the activities of this spirit around them.

PRAYERS OF DELIVERANCE

FROM THE SPIRIT OF ERROR

WORSHIP DECREE

On the altar of worship to Yahweh
The power of the Holy Ghost come down
The spirit of power come down
To consume the sacrifice of worship
Fire from heaven fall

MEDITATE

Jeremiah 10:11-17

Thus you shall say to them: "The gods that have not made the heavens and the earth shall perish from the earth and from under these heavens." He has made the earth by His power, He has established the world by His wisdom, And has stretched out the heavens at His discretion. When He utters His voice, There is a multitude of waters in the heavens: "And He causes the vapors to ascend from the ends of the earth. He makes lightning for the rain, He brings the wind out of His treasuries." Everyone is dull-hearted, without knowledge; Every metalsmith is put to shame by an image; For his molded image is falsehood, And there is no breath in them. They are futile, a work of errors; In the time of their punishment they shall perish. The Portion of Jacob is not like them, For He is the Maker of all things, And Israel is the tribe of His inheritance; The Lord of hosts is His name.

PRAYERS OF DELIVERANCE FROM THE SPIRIT OF ERROR

1. Lord Jesus, let your blood cleanse me from all my faults in the name of Jesus
2. Lord Jesus, let your hand uproot every time bomb of error planted in to my life in the name of Jesus
3. Connection of darkness linking me to the spirit of my error
4. Set me free from everything bringing error into my life.
5. Powers set to afflict me with the spirit of error, be destroyed in the name of Jesus.
6. The arrow of error shall not locate me in the name of Jesus
7. The arrow of error shall not located my spouse in the name of Jesus
8. The arrow of error shall not locate my children in the name of Jesus
9. The arrow of error shall not locate the works of my hand in the name of Jesus
10. The arrow of error shall not locate my endeavours in the name of Jesus
11. Father Lord, release the grace that overcomes error in the name of Jesus
12. The grace of God that silences error is released upon my life in the name of Jesus
13. Error in speech shall not be my portion,in the name of Jesus
14. Error in actions shall not be my portion, in the name of Jesus.
15. Small or big error is not my portion, in the name of Jesus
16. My testimony shall not be ruined with error, in the name of Jesus.
17. I shall not walk in errors, in the name of Jesus

18. My life is detached from the spirit of errors, in the name of Jesus
19. Lord Jesus, deliver me from the net of errors in the name of Jesus
20. Lord Jesus, deliver me from meandering errors and shame in the name of Jesus
21. All errors lurking at every corner to bring me down is destroyed by the power of the Lord Jesus in the name of Jesus.
22. I am set free from meadaring error and shame in the name of Jesus
23. Lord, uproot the spirit of error from my life in the name of Jesus.

JOURNAL

4

~

THE CURSE OF ABRUPT DEMOTION

The curse of Vashti is responsible for sudden fall from grace to grass. The curse of Vashti is responsible where an event occurs and brings a sudden fall to a woman who was once seated in high places with kings, princes and rulers.

Esther 1: 13-15

Then the king said to the wise men who understood the times (for this was the king's manner toward all who knew law and justice, those closest to him being Carshena, Shethar, Admatha, Tarshish, Meres, Marsena, and Memucan, the seven princes of Persia and Media, who had access to the king's presence, and who ranked highest in the kingdom): "What shall we do to Queen Vashti, according to law, because she did not obey the command of King

Ahasuerus brought to her by the eunuchs?" And Memucan answered before the king and the princes: "Queen Vashti has not only wronged the king, but also all the princes, and all the people who are in all the provinces of King Ahasuerus.

WHY THE FALL OF VASHTI IS SO RAPID?

There is a need for a quick fix for the behavior of Vashti for strong reasons. The answer is found below:

Esther 1: 16-20

And Memucan answered before the king and the princes: "Queen Vashti has not only wronged the king, but also all the princes, and all the people who are in all the provinces of King Ahasuerus. For the queen's behavior will become known to all women, so that they will despise their husbands in their eyes, when they report, 'King Ahasuerus commanded Queen Vashti to be brought in before him, but she did not come.' This very day the noble ladies of Persia and Media will say to all the king's officials that they have heard of the behavior of the queen. Thus there will be excessive contempt and wrath. If it pleases the king, let a royal decree go out from him, and let it be recorded in the laws of the Persians and the Medes, so that it will not be altered, that Vashti shall come no more before King Ahasuerus; and let the king give her royal position to another who is better than she. When the king's decree which he will make is proclaimed throughout all his empire (for it is great), all wives will honor their husbands, both great and small."

The spirit of Vashti, targets successful women for a reason. This spirit is well aware that these women occupy the topmost place in an institution, nation or establishment. This spirit also knows that many people, especially women, look up to them, as a result, the spirit seeks to penetrate the topmost woman in the establishment, so other women can emulate the works and activities of this destructive spirit manifested in her.
As a result of her influence, and to prevent mass pollution, the justice of God goes forth on the spirit of Vashti that perversion may be controlled and hindered.

The curse of Vashti attracts instant destruction because it is important for the influence of Vashti to be cut immediately so this spirit does not pollute mothers, subsequently families. The curse of Vashti is similar to the curse which plagued lucifer when he was cast out from heaven instantly, so he does not bring corruption into God's holy arena in heaven. Anytime a curse of Vashti is in operation, it calls forth for instant judgement.

HOW THE CURSE OF ABRUPT FALL MANIFESTS
#1 Dethronement
The curse of Vashti, when activated in the life of a woman, brings the most powerful people in the kingdom against her until she is dethroned. Dethronement may be spiritually or emotionally or even physically. Most times, God allows this curse to separate such women from the throne, so that they do not continue to use the authority of the throne to influence other vulnerable women.

#2 Judgements

31

When the curse of Vashti is activated, judgement rises up from places of power. This curse brings judgement from multiple angles of power upon the one who is under the influence of the spirit of Vashti. When the curse of Vashti is activated, the affected woman falls on the wrong side of the ordinances of God.

#3 Replacement or Absenteeism in Marriage

A powerful woman is rapidly taken out of a powerful situation and replaced. Some women could still be in their marriage but absente on the altar of their marriage in reality. This curse silences women in marriage. This curse is also responsible for the rise of another female spirit that influences the husband. This is sometimes manifested through adultery, when the husband is seeking an emotional replacement for the absent wife. This is sometimes manifested through emotional adultery where the husband settles all emotional matters with others but his wife. When this is at full play, divorce is one of the indicators of this spirit.

#4 Inability to Get Settled in Marriage: A young lady gets
a marriage proposal. She is being considered to become the destiny partner and wife of the man God has ordained for her. Though she silently desires the husband in her mind, but by the influence of the spirit of Vashti, manifested through pride, she says to the gentleman, "you cannot afford my lifestyle", "we do not belong to the same class", then the man leaves and finds another woman, and she waits and waits for the next man, and he never shows up, without knowing that she had just ridiculed the treasure in plain sight that the Lord sent her way.

The curse of Vashti is responsible for sudden fall from grace to grass. The curse of Vashti is responsible where an event occurs and brings a sudden fall to a woman who was once seated in high places with kings, princes and rulers.

PRAYERS OF DELIVERANCE FROM THE CURSE OF ABRUPT DEMOTION

WORSHIP DECREE

On the altar of worship to Yahweh
The power of the Holy Ghost come down
The spirit of power come down
To consume the sacrifice of worship
Fire from heaven fall

MEDITATE

Isaiah 14-12:-17

How you are fallen from heaven, O Lucifer, son of the morning! How you are cut down to the ground, You who weakened the nations! For you have said in your heart: 'I will ascend into heaven, I will exalt my throne above the stars of God; I will also sit on the mount of the congregation On the farthest sides of the north; I will ascend above the heights of the clouds, I will be like the Most High.' Yet you shall be brought down to Sheol, To the lowest depths of the Pit. "Those who see you will gaze at you, And consider you, saying: 'Is this the man who made the earth tremble, Who shook kingdoms, Who made the world as a wilderness And destroyed its cities, Who did not open the house of his prisoners?'

PRAYER OF DELIVERANCE FROM THE CURSE OF ABRUPT DEMOTION

1. Lord Jesus, forgive me for the times I ridiculed your glory for my life in the name of Jesus.
2. Thou curse of Vashti, responsible for marital delay, be broken by the blood of Jesus.
3. Thou curse of Vashti, responsible for barrenness in marriage, be broken by the blood of Jesus.
4. Thou curse of Vashti, responsible for abandonment in marriage, be broken by the blood of Jesus
5. Thou curse of Vashi, responsible for loneliness in marriage, be broken in the name of Jesus
6. Thou curse of Vashti, responsible for demotion in any area of my life, be broken in the name of Jesus.
7. Thou curse of Vashti, that is set to cast me into heaviness, be broken by the blood of Jesus
8. Thou curse of Vashti, that seeks to bring me into desolation, be broken in the name of Jesus
9. I shall not enter into the door of desolation in the name of Jesus
10. I shall not be susceptible to the spirit of Vashti in the name of Jesus
11. Thou spirit of Vashti, knocking on my door, let the fire of the Holy Spirit consume you in the name of Jesus
12. Thous spirit of Vashti, seeking to unleash the judgement of God against my life, receive the judgment of God in the name of jesus
13. My life shall not be susceptible to the spirit of Vashti in the name of Jesus.
14. I shall not fall from grace in the name of Jesus

15. I shall rise from grace to grace in the name of Jesus.

16. I shall not be absent in my marriage in the name of Jesus

17. I shall not be displaced in my marriage in the name of Jesus

18. I shall not be replaced on the altar of my marriage in the name of Jesus

19. I shall not be absent emotionally, spiritually, mentally, physically and financially in my marriage in the name of Jesus

20. Divorce shall not locate my marriage in the name of Jesus

21. My spouse shall not be absent from our marriage in the name of Jesus

22. Lord Jesus, override every cycle of demotion set in line for me in my marriage in the name of Jesus

23. Powers of failure assigned into my marriage is a failure in the name of Jesus.

24. Demotion, suddenly or slowly, is not my portion and my husband's portion in marriage in the name of Jesus

25. Martial failure that plagued my ancestors and the ancestors of my spouse, now manifesting in my marriage is canceled by the blood of Jesus

JOURNAL

5

~

THE CURSE OF MARITAL EXILE & DESOLATION

The curse of Vashti brings along two other curses: the curse of exile and desolation. This curse sends people into exile and desolation. The type of error this curse brings along positions the accursed into a situation where the only judgement cast against them is the judgement of exile and desolation.

MARITAL EXILE & DESOLATION

Marital exile casts people away from their marriage. This is when certain forces come into the marital space, and casts either of the spouses away from the marriage. Marital exile could be physically, financially, emotionally or spiritually. When marital exile and desolation occurs, all the resources that used to be available to the one whom the spirit of Vashti had taken over is no longer available, because she had been cast away, and access is taken away from her.

MANIFESTATION OF THE CURSE OF MARITAL EXILE AND DESOLATION

1. When the spirit of Vashti pushes a woman to trick a man into marriage. After the marriage, the veil of false humility is taken off, and when the man experiences his real bride, he enters into a mode of ignoring menttally, emotionally, spiritually, and may even abandon physically.

2. The curse of exile when activated dethrones the woman under the influence of the spirit of Vashti from her role as queen and wife.

3. When the curse of exile and desolation is activated, judgement rises up from places of power and the one under the influence of Vashti enters into a state of desolation in marriage or other places of influence.

4. The curse of desolation is at work in the life of a woman who had missed the spouse of destiny as a result of pride, and unable to get settled in marriage.

5. The curse of desolation is upon the woman who began to live in regret after leaving or abandoning her spouse.

6. The curse of desolation is manifested when the woman seeks companionship, but cannot find it because the companion of her youth had been chased away by the manifestation of the traits of Vashti.

7. The curse of desolation is manifested when the woman who had tormented her husband in their

sexual relations such that her husband no longer desires her sexually.

Departure from Marriage: The curse of desolation is manifested in certain circumstances when the husband had departed with a strange woman, leaving the wife behind.

Exile in Older Women:
The curse of marital exile and desolation is why some elderly women separate from their husband to go build a castle in the marriage of their children which eventually destroys the marriage of their children. In such situations, the exiled mother-in-law enters into war with her son's wife, wanting to become.

PRAYERS TO BREAK THE CURSE OF MARITAL EXILE AND DESOLATION

WORSHIP DECREE

On the altar of worship to Yahweh
The power of the Holy Ghost come down
The spirit of power come down
To consume the sacrifice of worship
Fire from heaven fall

MEDITATE

Isaiah 45: 11-13

Thus says the Lord, The Holy One of Israel, and his Maker: "Ask Me of things to come concerning My sons; And concerning the work of My hands, you command Me. I have made the earth, And created man on it. I—My hands—stretched out the heavens, And all their host I have commanded. I have raised him up in righteousness, And I will direct all his ways; He shall build My city And let My exiles go free, Not for price nor reward," Says the Lord of hosts.

PRAYERS TO BREAK THE CURSE OF MARITAL EXILE AND DESOLATION

1. Lord thank you for the power of revelation, in the name of Jesus
2. I shall not enter into marital exile in the name of Jesus

3. My husband shall not enter into marital exile in the name of Jesus

4. My household shall not enter into marital exile in the name of Jesus

5. Thou curse of desolation, be broken over my life by the blood of Jesus

6. Thou curse of exile, the blood of Jesus cancels you over my life in the name of Jesus

7. Thou curse of desolation is broken over my marital life in the name of jesus

8. The curse associated with false humility is broken over my life by the blood of Jesus.

9. The curse of exile shall not locate me in marriage in the name of Jesus

10. The curse of exile shall not locate my marriage in the name of Jesus

11. The curse of exile shall not locate my spouse in the name of Jesus.

12. The curse of exile and desolation at old age shall not locate me in the name of Jesus.

13. The curse that steals away companionship shall not locate my marriage in the name of Jesus

14. Lord heal my marriage on all sides in the name of Jesus.

15. Loneliness shall not locate my marriage in the name of Jesus.

16. Exile shall not locate my marriage in the name of Jesus.

17. No longer Will desolators know my way in the name of Jesus

18. No longer will my marriage attract the forces of desolation in the name of Jesus

19. The power of desolation that wants to empty my marriage is destroyed in the name of Jesus.
20. Desolation shall not find its way into my marriage in the name of Jesus
21. The garment of desolation is taken off my marriage in the name of Jesus.
22. The covenant of desolation against my marriage is broken by the blood of Jesus.
23. My marriage is delivered from the corridors and doorway into desolation, by the finger of God in the name of Jesus.
24. Desolation powers afflicting my marriage shall inherit their own desolation in the name of Jesus
25. Ordinance of deception controlling my marriage unto desolation, be shattered in the name of Jesus
26. Every curse of desolation in my foundation that is set to affect me in marriage is destroyed by the blood of Jesus
27. Thou power of desolation in my blood, fighting aggressively to destroy my marriage, be wiped off by the blood of Jesus

JOURNAL

ABOUT THE AUTHORS

Ebenezer Gabriels is an anointed Prophet, Worship Minister, Deliverance Minister and Intercessor for the nations. Abigail is a Pastor, Bible Teacher, Minstrel & Intercessor.

Ebenezer Gabriels and Abigail Gabriels are gifted technologists and have worked extensively in the areas of Computing and Data science.

Ebenezer and Abigail are involved in Church planting, were used the Pastors of LightHill Church - A worship-focused church USA. They are also involved in strategic 6-hour worship and national intercession movements. Their mandate is to revive worship altars and intercede for nations. Ebenezer is married to Abigail, and their lives are a testimony of the resurrection power and worship of the Lord,

Ebenezer Gabriels Ministries

ABOUT EGM

EGM provides resources for people to encounter Jesus. Our mandate is to revive dead worship altars, uproot rottenness from foundations, release God's people into Yahweh's worship, and intercede for the nations.

EGM's arm of publishing designs and develops Christian resources inspired by the Lord. EGM currently operates out of Gaithersburg in Maryland, USA.

CONTACT

Office/Mailing
19644 Club House Road Suite 815, Gaithersburg, Maryland, 20876 USA

hello@ebenezergabriels.org www.ebenezergabriels.org
Find Us on Social Media: @ebenezergabrielsministries

Similar Books from Ebenezer-Gabriels Ministries

UNCURSED

A PROPHETIC BOOK TO RAISE A CURSELESS GENERATION

Features
BACK-TO-THE-Womb
deliverance prayers

Prayers before, during &
after pregnancy

Prayers for babies in the
womb
And more

Ebenezer Gabriels
Abigail Gabriels

Marriage
Deliverance
Series

———

1

Deliverance from the yoke of

MARITAL IGNORANCE

A Prayer & Deliverance Manual for building Spiritual
Depth & A Blissful Marriage.

Ebenezer Gabriels
Abigail Gabriels

Pulling down the stronghold of

EVIL
PARTICIPANTS
IN MARRIAGE

A Prayer & Deliverance Manual for building Spiritual
Depth & a Blissful Marriage

Ebenezer Gabriels
Abigail Gabriels